PITCH

ALSO BY TODD BOSS

Yellowrocket

PITCH

poems

Todd Boss

W. W. NORTON & COMPANY

NEW YORK · LONDON

For information about permission to reproduce selections from this book,
write to Permissions, W. W. Norton & Company, Inc.,
500 Fifth Avenue, New York, NY 10110

For information about special discounts for bulk purchases, please contact
W. W. Norton Special Sales at specialsales@wwnorton.com or 800-233-4830

Manufacturing by Courier Westford
Book design by JAM Design
Production manager: Devon Zahn

Library of Congress Cataloging-in-Publication Data

Boss, Todd.
Pitch : poems / Todd Boss. — 1st ed.
p. cm.
ISBN 978-0-393-08103-9
I. Title.
PS3602.O8375P58 2011
811'.6—dc23
2011033286

ISBN 978-0-393-34552-0 pbk.

W. W. Norton & Company, Inc.
500 Fifth Avenue, New York, N.Y. 10110
www.wwnorton.com

W. W. Norton & Company Ltd.
Castle House, 75/76 Wells Street, London W1T 3QT

1 2 3 4 5 6 7 8 9 0

For my parents,
good people

Contents

IV

V

VI   Six Fragments for the 35W Bridge

VII

Acknowledgments

The author gratefully acknowledges the periodicals in which these poems first appeared:

Alaska Quarterly Review: "The Sky I Die By Will Be Grey"
Anthills: "Lordship"
Canteen: "Amen"
Dunes Review: "A Waltz for the Lovelorn"
Echoes: "To Wait"
Ecotone: "Your Dad Never Did, in the End,"
Georgia Review: "Despair Brings the Dog"; "My Dog Has No Nose"
Hampden-Sydney Poetry Review: "Today It Seemed I Had Nothing to Say"
Harvard Review Online: "The Ending Is in the Beginning"
Hawk & Whippoorwill: "The God of Our Farm Had Blades"
Knockout: "Marble Tumble Toys"; "Instrument"
Metro: "To Wait"
Michigan Quarterly Review: "And Then One Day in a Department Store"; "Blind"
Poetry: "Amidwives: Two Portraits"; "Call as You Will"; "Don't Be Flip"; "It Is Enough to Enter"; "Should Leash Laws"; "This Morning in a Morning Voice"; "Were I to Wring a Rag"; "The World Is in Pencil"
Subtropics: "Broke"

"Apple Slices" was commissioned by American Public Media for syndicated broadcast on *The Splendid Table* with Lynne Rossetto Kasper. "Luckenbach" and "Marble Tumble Toys" aired on Minnesota Public Radio's *All Things Considered.* Several of the poems in this book have been turned into animated shorts by various animation artists at Motionpoems.com.

This book was written with the support of a grant from the Minnesota State Arts Board and a residency at Ragdale from the Ragdale Foundation.

Pitch

It Is Enough to Enter

the templar
halls of museums, for

example, or
the chambers of churches,

and admire
no more than the beauty

there, or
remember the graveness

of stone, or
whatever. You don't

have to do any
better. You don't have to

understand
the liturgy or know history

to feel holy
in a gallery or presbytery.

It is enough
to have come just so far.

You need
not be opened any more

than does
a door, standing ajar.

and a rudder. All our acres
begged its pardon. Merest
breezes made its rusty flower
turn and whine and shudder.

Its wooden arm a weathered
stump, the god of our farm
no longer pumped the well
that once it lorded power over.

It belonged to another order.
On silent nights in summer,
windows open, many times
its vocal powers found me deep

in dreams and hauled me up.
Unearthly alarm! what ache!
How the vane would groan,
the rotor churn, and with what

moan when a good gust came!
It scared me to the bone, as if
some inner tower of my own
for an unknown water yearned.

We broke horses, broke
calves of their mothers'
milk, broke our hands
herding heifers, broke
axes and hammers right
off their hafts, broke
bread with thanks, broke
bank accounts, broke our
backs over banks of taters
and beets, broke beets
from their greens, broke
peas from their pods,
broke the silence of night
with a little something
spoke, broke necks of mice
that got in our traps, broke
the ice in the tank so the
stock could drink, broke
chickens with a twist
of fists, broke their yolks
into breakfasts, broke wide
our wallets for the offering
plate, broke the stitching
on our Bibles' spines, broke
harsh north winds with lines
of pines, and then, when
all was said and done, we
broke the bonds of earthly

toil when by our work we'd
been broke down, and,
over the soil that mended
where we lay, there ended
one, then broke another day.

—no matter how much
muscle I might have
mustered—my mother
was like to come along
behind me, reach around
me to take it up again
from where I'd left it,
lift it back into my line
of vision and in one
practiced motion from
that strangle in her bare
hands and thin air work
a second miraculous
stream of silver dishwash
into the day's last gleam . . .

        —eaten right
off the jackknife in
moons, half-moons,
quarter-moons and
crescents—
           still
summon common
summer afternoons
I spent as my dad's
jobsite grunt, framing
future neighbors'
houses out of 2x4s
and 4x6s,
           and our
brief and silent pick-
up tailgate lunch-
box lunch breaks
of link sausage,
longhorn cheddar,
larder pickles, cold
leftover roast-beef-
and-butter sandwiches
wrapped in paper,
a couple of pippins
from the Fall Crick
Pick 'n Save, and—
flavored of tin from
the lip of the cup

of a dented thermos
passed between us—
a hard-earned share
of still-chill well
water . . .
        Now
so many waned and
waxed moons later,
another well-paid,
well-fed, college-
bred paper-pusher, I
wonder that I've never
labored harder, nor
eaten better.

i. From farm to farm
    and one more
    midnight mile to go

    my father took
    too fast the last turn
    —on black ice—

    and presto,
    over the side of our half-
    ton Ford and into

    the drainway went my
    father's father's brother's
    turn-of-the-century Steinway

    piano. My mother's
    scream out-screamed
    the weather-alls—she

    cursed him, cursed him
    again, cursed him
    in the worst way, then

    cursed him in
    the first way again as we
    careened around

in a sudden Y
and our hi-beams
played

across the gleaming bed
of snowdrifted bramble
where it lay,

moaning chaotically
in every key,
miraculously

intact (yes,
miracles happen)
—only

scratched, in fact, one
foreleg broken.
And part of me

still sits on that bench seat,
as if on a line
above the stave, top-

heavy with gravity
and levity alike,
twisted, peering wake-

eyed through the melt-
blear scrawled across
the rear glass, trying

to pound it into my head
—the broken cords,
the empty bed—

while she let go,
Winter did,
her sheets and sheets

of December,
and started in
on January instead.

ii.   . . . and then two men
        in a Chevy Chevette
        show up, as if in a
        big top, and jump

        out to help, and some-
        how, between the
        three of them, they
        lift it from bed

        to bed, like an invalid
        or a comrade fallen.
        Two men with muscle
        enough for the un-

        planned rescue of a
        horizontal vertigrand—
        What are the chances
        of that? my mother

        years later still
        marvels, the chances
        of it seeming, when
        she says it, so slim,

        so remote, that even
        my father, narrow
        of shoulder, lean
        of arm, seems

saved by a whim
of grace. Was someone
watching us, through
the night's latched

louvers? It turns out
that the Lord's angels
—two of them, at least—
are piano movers.

iii. Fine

I wonder what it was like to have to call his dad on the phone the morning after and answer the question: *So, piano make it home all right?*

The thing was a loaner, after all, not a keeper, the elder farmer's finest stick of furniture. My dad had merely agreed to hold it for his older brother (my uncle), who played it but who'd moved too far away (Salt Lake) to take it.

It's difficult, caught short by a father, for any son to fake it, even over the phone. You go it alone.

It's like hitting a wrong note while rehearsing—the whole house hears it / has to try to hear through (and by hearing, heal) the broken melody line.

My father begins: *Oh, I think it's . . . probably . . . gonna be fine.*

iv. Pitch

Freud would say he did it on purpose—
 my father who couldn't hold a tune
if it had handles, reins,

          and a canvas
          shoulder harness—

that he towed the inscrutable implement
 a hundred miles and then,
on the last one,

          took a corner
          like a chance—

lifting his foot from pedal to pedal
 too late, too abruptly
to sustain the indelicate balance

          of instrument
          and machine—

and let the weighty symbol of his
 brother's favored status
as the family artist

          pitch—smashing it
          to bits by simply

giving it over—the Brahms, the Bach,
 and the Bartók—and if it's true,
if that's what he actually meant to do—

> to finally
> dramatically

silence that music, to ditch some child-
 hood inequality he's never spoken
candidly of, to measure

> the in-betweens
> in smithereens—

if it's true—it would open a lid, of a kind,
 on what treble and what bass things
are strung, one by one combined,

> in the dark
> wooden box

of his mind.

II

of this first movement of Suite
No. 3 in C major for solo

cello by Bach.
It's lovely and sad, how it

knows itself, knows its own
closing as it opens. Sad,

and also exhilarating,
how every moment of it

seems part of the ending,
how halfway through, you

get the feeling the ending
has long ago begun

so that as you're listening you
hear the work end, then end

again—then end another way
and another—then find

a new kind of ending and add
an ending to that ending that

seems to end things once
and for all—then fall

into what can only be the end
of endings. And you know it

when it comes, that final
finale. It comes about

like a hunger, like a thirst,
and it leaves no doubt.

You knew what to listen for
all along, as it turns out.

is no great

bread.
It's tough

and mostly
tasteless

stuff. You
chew

and chew.
It's said

to be good
for you, but

it only fills.
Swallow it,

it swells.
And it must

be mildly
sodiate,

for its last
effect is just

like its first:
thirst. Take

birth, for
instance:

nine whole
months

a baby
keeps mum.

Take spring:
up north,

all time's
a sandwich

between thick
white crusts

of wintering.
Take anything

that bakes,
brews, builds,

or makes
appointments

more than a
few days out.

Take worry
and doubt.

And what's
hurry but a

hurried wait?
Every day

we wait for
night; every

night we wait
for morning.

Take warning.
Take endings,

especially
endings made

unnecessarily
(or, worse,

by excess
drivel or a

swiveling
syntax,

superficially)
delayed:

the wait
is what

a writer
spends

his brief
and bitter

tenure on
this breath-

taking, heart-
breaking

earth
making

every
ending

worth.

One day the doctor tells you that you're blind
to the truth. It's physical; something about
the retina, rods and cones. Truth is a wave-
length in the spectrum you're unable to detect.
All your life you've been compensating,
  convincing yourself you could see what you
could not. Suddenly you've got questions
  about religion and politics and art, but what
you finally ask is about treatment. *No,* he says,
  there's little medical science can do. We know
it might be genetic; it's likely one or another
  of your parents can't see the truth any better
than you. Also, we know this condition tends
  to grow more acute with age. But frankly,
what doesn't? he says, trying a smile. Well,
  that does it, you think to yourself, as you
press the button in the elevator that will
  drop you gently to the ground. Your wife
and kids were right all along, as were your
  friends, who spent their lives dispensing
advice you repeatedly waved away. In a way,
  it's a relief, isn't it. Now you can get down
to the business of apologizing, to everyone,
  for what has been in fact an honest disability,
one that shouldn't keep you from, say, driving
  a car, but which has gradually and progressively
made you the truth-less husk of a man you
  always knew, somehow, at your core, that you
are.

—not pen. It's got
that same silken
dust about it, doesn't it,
that same sense of
having been roughed
onto paper even
as it was planned.
It had to be a labor
of love. It must've
taken its author some
time, some shove.
I'll bet it felt good
In the hand—the *o*
of the ocean, and
the *and* and the *and*
of the land.

infinitesimally contain
that feather-light glean
of magnetite that can't
but lean toward home?
Or does it, as a whale's
does, scroll a roll of in-
visible paper under its
sonar's tetchy needle-
pens? Does it resemble,
as a bee's will seasonally,
the nimblest of digital
buzz-cams whose aims
train on the horizon's
undulate forms? Or is
one's dog's homing
orientation a function
not of brains but of some
burden on the brawn,
a nagging itch, a hip
dysplasia, a kink one
can't just think away, to
which an arrow in one's
marrow is mindlessly
drawn? Is *home* in fact
bodily, an ache to the
amputee to which he—
should the lost limb fall
or seem to fall asleep—
will repeatedly wake, to
shake the feeling free—?

43

—retracing
trail until

the sun makes
up its mind

to leave
a wilderness

behind—you'll
never find

the dog
who seems

(in this most
vivid of vivid

dreams) alive
and fresh,

a wish
made flesh,

who left
the leash

and now is
lost—lost

good in the
heart's deep

wood.

III

Joke

My mother used to say,
Nobody was here today
and she made dinner.

The joke was weird,
for where was Nobody
now, and where

the feast prepared?

i. A Wife Will Wean

by coming between

her husband
and the woman who

whelped him. And
should he bemoan

the sweet taste gone,
she'll boast of how she

helped him—helped
him get beyond

his milks at last, and cut
from gums beneath

—the better to shake
her memory with—

permanent teeth.

ii. A Mother Will Woo

a married man who

was once her darling
son. She can't conceive

of anyone loving him
through and through

as she has done. She'll
do whatever it takes

to test his trust. She'll
run a tempered blade

into the marriage
bed and find the naked

place where she was
most betrayed

—and thrust.

The day
we agreed

to need no
third

you poured
a bath and

came to
terms.

The spirit,
you said,

of the un-
conceived

(not soul,
but some

Unheard
that grieved

for a soul)
now grieved

for the letting
go.

are no minor

marvels, as

minors and

seniors alike

by their

rapt attention

repeatedly

prove. And

much as

I tend to nag

my wife

for bagging up

more and

more battery-

op noise-

making

toys at Toys

"R" Us, I

must admit I'm

a bit of a

sucker

for the cyclical,

metrical

ritual of a

mechanical

redundancy.

Drop a

ball and watch it

frustrate

gravity's pull

                          upon it, till
it fumbles
                   to the carpet;
I'll find
                       it's taken all
my
                 wits along with it.
And
                       even a tin ear
for music
                    can appreciate
the kilter
                      clavier tickle,
the zig-
                    zag and fickle
clock-
                    work of a cat's
eye as it
                         stumbles
through a
                       mousetrap
rigging down,
                      down and
down. Tell me,
                      honestly,
which of us—
                     what saint,
what sinner—
                       doesn't
love to see a

                    steely strike
a bumper
                    or a spinner
in the blink-
                    ing inner
din and careen
                    of a pin-
ball machine;
                    or hear a bell
clang
                    when a muscle-
man fresh
                    from the bull
pen gives
                    'em all hell
on the mid-
                    way with a
hard haul
                    on a ball-
peen hammer;
                    or feel,
as if by
                    force of will,
the call
                    of a winning
number
                    in the somber
lull
                    that falls
after the metal

                    hamster
wheel of a bingo
                         creel
squeals to
                    another stop?
Step right
                         up, folks,
every
                    player is a winner.
Last
                    night I won big when
a
                         payout came in on
an
                    earlier play I'd made
for
                         forgiveness for
being up-
                         tight about
the steady
                         toy-sized
leak in my
                         wife's wallet.
Last week
                         I said, *What
the heck,*
                         let down my
rinky-
                    dink guard like
a gate,

                        got a little bit
tipsy on a
                        lowball full
of Kentucky
                        bourbon
whiskey like a
                        frisky
suburban cowboy,
                        sat
up late on eBay,
                        and
bought my wife
                        a blast
from her past:
                        the nine-
teen seventy-six
                        Schaper
game Tumble
                        Bug, mint
in the box.
                        The UPS man
brought it
                        yesterday. Let
me tell you
                        how it works:
A handful
                        of colored
kilter beans,
                        wobbling
loosely, filters

                    nimbly
down a
                    jump-studded
track to a
                    plastic tray.
It's oddly
                    pleasing, I've
got to say.
                    And you
should've seen
                    her face
light up!
                    There must
be something
                    powerful
at work in
                    such play.
I say a well-
                    wrought
thought ought
                    to run
that way.
                    Love, too,
clicks neatly
                    when give
and take are
                    calibrated
correctly:
                    Along my own
rickety

                    boardwalk of a
romance,
                    for instance,
my
                    embarrassingly
rocky
                    history
of finding my
                    groove
seemed ill-fated
                    last
week, yet at

midnight last night I got lucky.

—Let me taste
the kitchen in your skin.

Now that company's gone
& the kids are tucked in,
let the real feasting begin.

Let me lay you out on the
bed like a spread of bone

china. —Yes, I want a
piece of you.
    Yes, I do.

Give me your garlic, and
the sting of your pepper.

The plenty of your hair
(cinnamon, cardamom).

Here a hint of coffee, &
there, in the cup of your
shoulder, I swear, a lick
of salted butter.
    But first:
your wrist, your palm's
sweet meat.
   Dip your
fingers in my kisses—
star anise—lemon zest—

Say a grace, my fare,
my flight,
               & let's re-light
the candles tonight.

grand . . . would you mind terribly, my groundling,
if I compared it to the *Hindenburg* (I mean,
before it burned)—that vulnerable, elephantine

dream of transport, a fabric *Titanic* on an ocean
of air? There: with binoculars, dear, you can
just make me out, in a gondola window, wildly

flapping both arms as the ship's shadow
moves like a vagrant country across the
country where you live in relative safety. I pull

that oblong shadow along behind me wherever
I go. It is so big, and goes so slowly, it alters
ground temperatures noticeably, makes

housewives part kitchen curtains, wrings
whimpers from German shepherds. Aren't I
ridiculous? Isn't it anachronistic, this

dirigible devotion, this Zeppelin affection, a moon
that touches, with a kiss of wheels, the ground
you take for granted beneath your heels?—

IV

buy,
fix up,
move into,

and die
in an abandoned
country

church, town
hall, or bell-and-
flagpole school the way
he always said he

would, though he'd
spent a lifetime
pointing them out
where they

stood, too fallen
to be proud, but still
high
along some South
Dakota ridge or
Nebraska plain on a

family drive—
There's a
beauty,
he'd say almost
inaudibly,
and, farther down
the highway,

sigh.

All Summer That Summer the Saturday Daylight

                poured in, over
the starboard rim of my
neighbor's dented Duracraft,

over-poured it, then poured
even more over the port side
(astern, on a rope tied

to a seat: a milk jug thick
with the milk of concrete)
while under, in the shallows

between trailer and tar,
her shadow slid sideways
from deep within his un-

mown lawn at dawn till far
across my grass to my car
as afternoon passed

into dusk.
Then: click!—automatic
lights all over town in front

of lit and unlit homes alike
were tricked into life again,
and silver-white moths came

nibbling nibbling—starving
all night—till they dropped
like feather-winged weights

into darkness, from flight.

govern

a canine

meeting,

their paws

all over

instinct's

greeting,

it's we

who do

the dancing

there, lest

our restraints

ourselves

ensnare.

Over the head,

between

the legs,

we tangle

with our

rules

& regs

like film

in a projector's

cogs,

reclaim

the lead,

then blame

the dogs.

i. A Stock Homily

is all Aunt

Emily got.
God's proxy

didn't know
the family,

so her lot
of holy elegy

from pulpit
and at plot

had about it
an anonymity

that felt like
sin

to those
whose pages

her life was
written in.

ii. Cairn

Can
of paint
on can
on can.

A handy
man un-
done and
gone.

Never did
Amen
go on
so thin.

iii. Amen

and *amen,*
and again
and again
amen, cry
the wren and
the wren's
hundred
kindred from
the farm's
elms' arms,
while the
dried-up
acre of un-
taken corn
along the
long-ago
overgrown
driveway
wonders,
Who is lord?
Who is lord?
Who is lord
over us?

It took five metropolitan airports
to bring my mom and dad and
my sister and me with our kids—
three generations—together again
for our first family vacation in
years. Our ears were still ringing
as we untangled the ropy wrangle
of roadway out of San Antonio
and into Hill Country, where,
after three days of seeing what
the guidebook said we had to see,
my sister finally persuaded us
to hit the sticks off Ranch Road
1376 until our rental cars rocked
to a stop in a gravel lot beside a
weathered shack in a thick shade
made famous in that country song
called
             Luckenbach, Texas.
                         At most
a ghost of a ghost of a ghost town,
a stable of well-broke picnic tables,
a platform stage, and a dance hall
patched with tin . . . it wasn't much,
but as the sign by the roadside said,
it was good enough for anybody
to be somebody in.
                     We sat down.
The kids ran around. We found us
four Shiner Bocks at the bar in

the rear of the shack where some
white-haired boys were picking the
Atkins, Robbins and Ritters out of
their Fenders, Gibsons and Taylors.
We could almost feel the pegs un-
twisting the tensions in our shoulders.
We started dropping *g*'s from our
i-n-g's. You are here, said our inner
locators—right here. Something
earthen was in the air. My sister
pushed her sunglasses up into her
hair, and grinned at me like I was
her brother.

      And brother, I don't
care how slick you are, there's a
hick in you somewhere, some
folkie in a tie-dyed T. You don't
belong in your dead-end job any
more than we belonged in that
dead-end town, but we pick our
dead-ends in the end, don't we,
friend?

      My mom and dad don't
farm anymore; my sister
manages info-tech. And as for me,
I live in a city, a pitch-man for
the rich man, a fast-track flak.
Only recently have I begun
to let my small-town
farm roots show.

      I've been a fool.

But as our cars ticked cool under
Luckenbach's moon in the crazy
calm of that afternoon, and the
roosters crowed, and the whole
hollow glowed in a sepia haze . . .
it seemed our ghosts, at last
restored, out amongst the ghosts
of that ghost town poured, and,
hitching up their things, got down
to the dizzying business of two-
stepping up the fence-posted avenue,
and around and down through
leaves past the washer-pitching
pits to the creek, cheek to cheek,
to the music ghosts love most—

And now I can say it like I knew it
all along: That crick in your neck
is the heck you've got from being
somebody you're not.
              But that's
okay, 'cause as the old folks say:
Somewhere they're playing your song.

and honky-tonk piano, is it. Life's
got a little more

cello to it. The rough chew of
horsehair trying to flow

through wire. The bow of bale
on woe. I know. I hear it too.

And I'm right there with you,
in the dance hall dark. I'll

hold your hand while we wait,
if you want me to. We can

sway or not sway, either way.
These others, let them

figure every day for a jig, a thrill
of middles, a dizzy

swish of hems. As for us, our
attention's on the man

sitting stage-side, his brim low
over his eyes, waiting

his turn. Soon, it'll rise
from its case like a zombie

and he'll sit down beside it
with his arm around it

and with his other arm
draw from within its dusty frame

a conversation so slowly
healing from the broken, we'll

recognize it in our bones. Hell,
this old hall, if it could feel,

would feel it in the hewn
beams above us and below.

Don't go, it'll say, in its
low romantic way. Don't

go. Stay and dance some more.
But the piano player

will have already gone
with the woman he's had his

eye on all along, and
the fiddle player won't know

this song, and some crew-cut boy
with his cotton shirt

wet through will scoff, *Who died?*
and lead his friends

off toward a quarter of town
where they're still pouring neon

over gin. That's when we'll turn
to one another, won't we,

and wordlessly begin.
For this is what we're here for,

aren't we, dear. The rake of every
rust-red sound going down

with a shudder, like the call
of the loon across the lake, or like

whiskey, warm and at the same
time cold.

And I'll hold you to me
gently, move you gently

around the floor, and gently
tell you you're all the more lovely

now you are old.

V

for beauty. She
knows not where it

nests, nor how it
flushes and goes,
nor how best

to close it
in her mouth's
soft wallet, nor

whether, if she
brought it and
laid it at the feet

of her lord, he'd
mete out any but
the usual reward.

when you drop
your mate at
the dock or

your children
at school. Don't
be cool. Don't

be coy. Or if
you do, don't
assume it's

okay to act
that way. For
today may

be your last
chance at
joy before it

flashes away
like a tin
toy in one of

those shooting
galleries in
midways: those

ducks that seem
to paddle a
stream that's

not a stream
but a rotating
axle,

toothed for
disappearance
& reappearance,

a spit
without point
or flame,

along which
randomly clucks
the whole game.

He cried at everything.
We all got used to it.

Holding a baby.
Reciting the doxology.
Driving alone through columns of sunlight.
Something somebody said on the assembly line.

He did not convulse.
He did not whimper.

It was like a spring inside of him.
The tears just gleamed forth like gems.
They splotched his shirtfronts.
They dotted the table.

He did not appear to be embarrassed.
If you asked what was wrong, he said *Nothing*.
It was beautiful, how he let it come.
How he let it go.

He expressed no wish for company.
Still you couldn't help it.
Considering your own dry eyes.

piano
 and played
no tune,

but laid
both hands

along that board
 of soundless
flats and

bones and
up and down

in a fumble
 of wooden
knuckles

found
the distant

murmurings
 their hammers
made

on strings
a fitting

trade
 for the nearer
clatter

of her
wedding

rings.

From a farmhouse,
a farm looks like

work.
Does God too,

instead of a blue
planet rolling

in splendor,
see only lists

of things to do?
Is He a builder

or merely
a mender, now

his dreams
of lordship

are all come
true?

And Then One Day in a Department Store

in a faraway city
it will come to you, the strains
of some Schumann or Chopin
you'd forgotten your father
used to fumble over all
those years before, and you'll

realize—without quite
realizing it—how beautiful it is,
and that your father did well
to play it Sunday afternoon
after Sunday afternoon until
he'd pressed the limits
of his skills to its service,

and menswear will steadily
drift away as though it—not
you—were on the escalator,
and the third floor will come
gently to rest in the first and
vice versa, and somewhere in
housewares, or jewelry maybe,

as the last cascades of notes
come unstrung from memory
and melt into the past, you'll
feel what he felt—or feel again
that familiar longing to learn—.
But it will be over too soon,
and there will be no return.

VI

SIX FRAGMENTS FOR THE 35W BRIDGE

1

My
cousin
called
from
across
town
the
hour
the
bridge
went
down.
Are
you
okay?
Fine,
fine,
I
said.
Good-bye,
Good-bye.
The
call
went
dead.
But
I
love

my
cousin.
So
I
held
the
line.

2

Like
reading,
crossing
suspends
us
beginning
to
end.
We
must
trust
rusting
trusses
and
rumble
over
crumbling
concrete
and
abstract
constructions,
minding
marginal
dashes
that
flash
past
fast,

first
to
last,
a
slip
of
fishes.

3

Alaskan
awhile,
I'll
never
forget
pulling
myself
in
cabled
handcart
to
McCarthy
over
glacial
roar
from
shore
to
shore,
that
tin
trap
less
car
than
lift
chair,
the

cable
less
cable
than
schism
of
air.

4

Once
we
were
Brooklyn
Bridge
sore.
Now
we
lay
rebar
and
pour.
Me,
I
have
Whitman
and
Frost.
And
you?
From
what
lone
mossed
monument
of
stone
did

you
come
so
far
to
be
lost?

5

Not
water
but
air's
where
the
fallen
fall
first.
Not
landing
but
numbing
to
the
fact
that
landing
is
coming
is
the
worst
part
of
falling.
Not
losing

a
loved
one
but
calling
and
calling.

6

Catching
something
sunken,
the
black
river
flings
back
one
white
wave
riding
forever,
neither
gaining
nor
losing,
a
bird's
lost
breast
feathers,
a
wrinkled
white
kerchief,
the
black

stream
seeming
blacker
against
the
shoreline
birches.

VII

The Sky I Die By Will Be Grey

and warm, and I

will walk all day
the icy Mississippi till my

little weight
on that great wintry way shocks

—with a thick
crack deep and sharp—a flock

of one of the more
inconsequential birds on

shore,
shakes them out of the woods' core

like a shook rug shakes dried specks
of mud

into the air. They'll whirl awhile there before

they settle—swirling as a soul
might swirl

between worlds, in a light too slight,
and on

too sharply cold a night
to fly by.

—sure as whistling,
sure as the can opener's
little shrug and shudder
or the mailman's motor.

As though woe's name
were her own, she collies
to its border, tail tamped
under. All over town,

tears, however made, are
on her radar as if misery
led the pack, its track
invisible to all but one

whose own nose
is low enough to snow
to know what it knows,
and how it goes, alone.

Below the ongoing woe of his bow on strings,
    if you crank up the volume,
        the cellist himself becomes

audible, shuddering air in / out in great spasms,
    as if his lungs were keen
        to break into the song

his arms / wrists / fingertips ply, or as if his cello
    weren't just between
        his knees but in

his loafers / wearing his coat and tie. No wonder
    it's so human, what he offers:
        He wills / he

suffers the cello into being. Or is it *him* providing,
    by dint of so steady / so
        faithful a union, the cello's

other body / the one that does its wanting / loving?
    And we,
        so used to the notion

that music is made of wood / wire / horsehair / pin,
    we recall: a cello
        is only a voice box after all—

that the one surrounding it with elbows / torso / chin,
    is the real instrument
        the work resonates in—

and that everything man makes is an aspirant song
    sawn across / along
        a deeper grain within.

to beat the froggiest
of morning voices,
  my boy gets out of bed
and takes a lumpish song
  along—a little lyric
learned in kindergarten,
  something about a
boat. He's found it in
  the bog of his throat
before his feet have hit
  the ground, follows
its wonky melody down
  the hall and into the loo
as if it were the most
  natural thing for a little
troubadour to do, and lets
  it loose awhile in there
to a tinkling sound while
  I lie still in bed, alive
like I've never been, in
  love again with life,
afraid they'll find me
  drowned here—drowned
in more than my fair
  share of joy.

Like foot-worn wooden floors
 that ache in common places,
the hearts of the lovelorn groan

 as, through their paces, again
and again their roomers pass.
 Isn't there a music—strings—

in the way an old floor sings?
 And oh, but to leave our porches
and step into the grass! to bear

 on our shoulders no more
than moonlight, and to settle,
 suspended awhile!—to smile

at the weightlessness of things—
 as children do,
                on swings—

that hadn't been said already—
my head full of moldy
hay and feelings
of futility—

until you asked me
what it was like, for a change,
to have no barred owl
brooding above the barn,

and so I went stealing again,
softly, softly
up the worn wood loft ladder,
hoping to startle up
a glimpse of something

that even now might heft
itself lightly through the mouth
of the mow, and drift just
out of view, off-levelly,
all hollow and feather pillow,

folding and unfolding
and folding itself silently into
the forest where its terrible
utility moves like a shudder
over every living thing.

Notes

"Cairn" was cowritten with Jack Miles in memory of Ed Crowder.

"Six Fragments for the 35W Bridge" is part of a 35-piece project to commemorate the fifth anniversary of the August 2007 collapse of the 35W Bridge in Minneapolis. The sixth fragment here is taken almost verbatim from Robert Frost's poem "West-Running Brook."